50 Chocolate Baked Dishes

By: Kelly Johnson

Table of Contents

- Chocolate Cake
- Brownies
- Chocolate Chip Cookies
- Chocolate Muffins
- Chocolate Lava Cake
- Chocolate Croissants
- Chocolate Cheesecake
- Chocolate Soufflé
- Chocolate Pound Cake
- Chocolate Tart
- Chocolate Éclairs
- Chocolate Babka
- Chocolate Donuts
- Chocolate Mousse Cake
- Chocolate Swiss Roll
- Chocolate Scones
- Chocolate Rugelach
- Chocolate Biscotti
- Chocolate Bread Pudding

- Chocolate Danish
- Chocolate Fudge Bars
- Chocolate Shortbread
- Chocolate Whoopie Pies
- Chocolate Macarons
- Chocolate Churros
- Chocolate Pecan Pie
- Chocolate Pavlova
- Chocolate Madeleine
- Chocolate Peanut Butter Bars
- Chocolate Truffle Tart
- Chocolate Meringue Pie
- Chocolate Torte
- Chocolate Zucchini Bread
- Chocolate Sticky Buns
- Chocolate Bread
- Chocolate Crinkle Cookies
- Chocolate Almond Cake
- Chocolate Marbled Pound Cake
- Chocolate Biscuit Cake
- Chocolate Roll Cake

- Chocolate Cupcakes
- Chocolate Oatmeal Cookies
- Chocolate Banana Bread
- Chocolate Pretzel Bites
- Chocolate Puff Pastry Twists
- Chocolate Bundt Cake
- Chocolate Cinnamon Rolls
- Chocolate Raspberry Bars
- Chocolate Dipped Biscotti
- Chocolate Marshmallow Brownies

Dark Indulgence

Ingredients:

- 1 cup (240ml) hot coffee
- 1 cup (240ml) milk
- ½ cup (120ml) vegetable oil
- 2 eggs
- 2 tsp vanilla extract
- 2 cups (250g) all-purpose flour
- 2 cups (400g) sugar
- ¾ cup (75g) unsweetened cocoa powder
- 2 tsp baking powder
- 1½ tsp baking soda
- 1 tsp salt

Instructions:

1. Preheat oven to 350°F (175°C). Grease and flour two 9-inch round cake pans.
2. In a large bowl, whisk together flour, sugar, cocoa powder, baking powder, baking soda, and salt.
3. Add eggs, milk, oil, and vanilla. Beat on medium speed until combined.
4. Stir in hot coffee until the batter is smooth (it will be thin).
5. Divide batter evenly between prepared pans.
6. Bake for 30-35 minutes, or until a toothpick inserted in the center comes out clean.
7. Let cakes cool in pans for 10 minutes, then transfer to a wire rack to cool completely.

8. Frost as desired and enjoy!

Brownies

Ingredients:

- 1 cup (225g) unsalted butter, melted
- 2 cups (400g) sugar
- 4 eggs
- 2 tsp vanilla extract
- 1 cup (125g) all-purpose flour
- ¾ cup (75g) unsweetened cocoa powder
- ½ tsp salt
- ½ tsp baking powder

Instructions:

1. Preheat oven to 350°F (175°C). Grease a 9x13-inch baking pan.
2. In a large bowl, whisk melted butter and sugar until smooth.
3. Add eggs and vanilla, mixing well.
4. Sift in flour, cocoa powder, salt, and baking powder. Stir until just combined.
5. Pour batter into the prepared pan and spread evenly.
6. Bake for 25-30 minutes, or until a toothpick comes out with a few moist crumbs.
7. Let cool before slicing.

Chocolate Chip Cookies

Ingredients:

- 1 cup (225g) unsalted butter, softened
- 1 cup (200g) brown sugar
- ½ cup (100g) sugar
- 2 eggs
- 2 tsp vanilla extract
- 2½ cups (315g) all-purpose flour
- 1 tsp baking soda
- ½ tsp salt
- 2 cups (340g) chocolate chips

Instructions:

1. Preheat oven to 350°F (175°C). Line a baking sheet with parchment paper.
2. Cream together butter, brown sugar, and sugar until light and fluffy.
3. Add eggs and vanilla, mixing until combined.
4. Stir in flour, baking soda, and salt. Mix until just combined.
5. Fold in chocolate chips.
6. Scoop dough onto the baking sheet, spacing 2 inches apart.
7. Bake for 10-12 minutes, until edges are golden brown.
8. Let cool on the sheet for 5 minutes, then transfer to a wire rack.

Chocolate Muffins

Ingredients:

- 1¾ cups (220g) all-purpose flour
- ½ cup (50g) unsweetened cocoa powder
- 1 cup (200g) sugar
- 2 tsp baking powder
- ½ tsp salt
- ½ cup (120ml) milk
- ½ cup (120ml) vegetable oil
- 2 eggs
- 1 tsp vanilla extract
- 1 cup (170g) chocolate chips

Instructions:

1. Preheat oven to 375°F (190°C). Line a muffin tin with paper liners.
2. In a large bowl, whisk together flour, cocoa powder, sugar, baking powder, and salt.
3. In another bowl, mix milk, oil, eggs, and vanilla.
4. Combine wet and dry ingredients, stirring until just mixed.
5. Fold in chocolate chips.
6. Divide batter evenly into the muffin cups.
7. Bake for 18-20 minutes, until a toothpick comes out clean.
8. Let cool in the pan for 5 minutes before transferring to a wire rack.

Chocolate Lava Cake

Ingredients:

- ½ cup (115g) unsalted butter
- 4 oz (115g) dark chocolate, chopped
- 2 eggs
- 2 egg yolks
- ¼ cup (50g) sugar
- 2 tbsp all-purpose flour

Instructions:

1. Preheat oven to 425°F (220°C). Grease four ramekins and dust with cocoa powder.
2. Melt butter and chocolate together, stirring until smooth.
3. In a separate bowl, whisk eggs, egg yolks, and sugar until pale and thick.
4. Gently fold in melted chocolate and flour.
5. Divide batter between ramekins.
6. Bake for 10-12 minutes, until edges are set but centers are soft.
7. Let cool for 1 minute, then invert onto plates and serve immediately.

Chocolate Croissants

Ingredients:

- 1 sheet puff pastry, thawed
- ½ cup (90g) chocolate chips
- 1 egg (for egg wash)

Instructions:

1. Preheat oven to 375°F (190°C). Line a baking sheet with parchment paper.
2. Roll out puff pastry and cut into triangles.
3. Place chocolate chips at the wide end of each triangle.
4. Roll tightly from the wide end to the tip.
5. Brush with egg wash.
6. Bake for 15-18 minutes until golden brown.
7. Let cool before serving.

Chocolate Cheesecake

Ingredients:

- 2 cups (200g) chocolate cookie crumbs
- ½ cup (115g) melted butter
- 24 oz (680g) cream cheese, softened
- 1 cup (200g) sugar
- 3 eggs
- 8 oz (225g) melted dark chocolate
- 1 tsp vanilla extract
- ½ cup (120ml) heavy cream

Instructions:

1. Preheat oven to 325°F (160°C). Grease a 9-inch springform pan.
2. Mix cookie crumbs with melted butter and press into the pan.
3. Beat cream cheese and sugar until smooth.
4. Add eggs one at a time, mixing well.
5. Stir in melted chocolate, vanilla, and heavy cream.
6. Pour into the crust and bake for 55-60 minutes.
7. Cool completely before refrigerating for at least 4 hours.

Chocolate Soufflé

Ingredients:

- 4 oz (115g) dark chocolate, chopped
- 2 tbsp (30g) butter
- 2 tbsp (30g) flour
- ½ cup (120ml) milk
- 2 egg yolks
- 2 egg whites
- 2 tbsp (25g) sugar

Instructions:

1. Preheat oven to 375°F (190°C). Grease and sugar ramekins.
2. Melt chocolate and butter together.
3. Stir in flour, then gradually add milk.
4. Remove from heat and mix in egg yolks.
5. Beat egg whites with sugar until stiff peaks form.
6. Gently fold egg whites into the chocolate mixture.
7. Fill ramekins and bake for 12-15 minutes.

Chocolate Pound Cake

Ingredients:

- 1 cup (225g) butter, softened
- 2 cups (400g) sugar
- 4 eggs
- 1 tsp vanilla extract
- 1¾ cups (220g) all-purpose flour
- ½ cup (50g) cocoa powder
- ½ tsp salt
- ½ cup (120ml) milk

Instructions:

1. Preheat oven to 350°F (175°C). Grease a loaf pan.
2. Cream butter and sugar until fluffy.
3. Add eggs one at a time, then vanilla.
4. Mix flour, cocoa, and salt, then add alternately with milk.
5. Pour into pan and bake for 60-70 minutes.

Chocolate Tart

Ingredients:

- 1½ cups (180g) flour
- ½ cup (115g) butter, cold
- ¼ cup (50g) sugar
- 1 egg yolk
- 2 tbsp cold water
- 8 oz (225g) dark chocolate
- 1 cup (240ml) heavy cream

Instructions:

1. Preheat oven to 350°F (175°C). Mix flour, butter, and sugar until crumbly.
2. Add egg yolk and water, form dough, and press into a tart pan.
3. Bake for 15 minutes.
4. Heat heavy cream and pour over chopped chocolate. Stir until smooth.
5. Pour into tart shell and refrigerate for 2 hours.

Chocolate Éclairs

Ingredients:

- ½ cup (120ml) water
- ¼ cup (56g) butter
- ½ cup (60g) flour
- 2 eggs
- 1 cup (240ml) heavy cream
- 2 tbsp sugar
- 4 oz (115g) melted chocolate

Instructions:

1. Preheat oven to 400°F (200°C). Boil water and butter, then stir in flour.
2. Add eggs one at a time, mixing well.
3. Pipe onto a baking sheet and bake for 25 minutes.
4. Whip heavy cream with sugar and fill éclairs.
5. Dip tops in melted chocolate.

Chocolate Babka

Ingredients:

- 2½ cups (315g) flour
- ¼ cup (50g) sugar
- 1 tsp yeast
- ½ cup (120ml) milk
- 2 eggs
- 4 tbsp (56g) butter
- 4 oz (115g) melted chocolate

Instructions:

1. Mix flour, sugar, and yeast.
2. Add milk, eggs, and butter, kneading into dough.
3. Let rise for 1 hour, then roll out and spread melted chocolate.
4. Roll up, twist, and place in a loaf pan.
5. Bake at 350°F (175°C) for 35-40 minutes.

Chocolate Donuts

Ingredients:

- 1½ cups (190g) flour
- ½ cup (50g) cocoa powder
- 1 tsp baking powder
- ½ cup (100g) sugar
- ½ cup (120ml) milk
- 1 egg
- 2 tbsp butter, melted
- 4 oz (115g) melted chocolate (for glaze)

Instructions:

1. Preheat oven to 350°F (175°C). Grease a donut pan.
2. Mix flour, cocoa, baking powder, and sugar.
3. Add milk, egg, and butter, stirring until smooth.
4. Fill pan and bake for 10-12 minutes.
5. Dip in melted chocolate.

Chocolate Mousse Cake

Ingredients:

- 1 cup (150g) crushed chocolate cookies
- ¼ cup (56g) melted butter
- 8 oz (225g) dark chocolate, melted
- 2 cups (480ml) heavy cream
- ¼ cup (50g) sugar
- 1 tsp vanilla extract

Instructions:

1. Mix cookie crumbs with melted butter and press into a pan.
2. Whip heavy cream with sugar until soft peaks form.
3. Fold in melted chocolate and vanilla.
4. Pour over crust and chill for 4 hours.

Chocolate Swiss Roll

Ingredients:

- ¾ cup (95g) all-purpose flour
- ¼ cup (25g) cocoa powder
- 1 tsp baking powder
- ¼ tsp salt
- 4 eggs
- ¾ cup (150g) sugar
- 1 tsp vanilla extract
- 2 tbsp vegetable oil
- ½ cup (120ml) heavy cream
- 4 oz (115g) melted dark chocolate

Instructions:

1. Preheat oven to 375°F (190°C). Line a baking sheet with parchment paper.
2. Whisk flour, cocoa, baking powder, and salt together.
3. Beat eggs and sugar until thick and pale.
4. Stir in vanilla and oil, then fold in dry ingredients.
5. Spread batter evenly into pan and bake for 10-12 minutes.
6. Turn out onto a clean towel, roll up while warm, and cool.
7. Whip cream and fold in melted chocolate.
8. Unroll cake, spread filling, and roll up again.

Chocolate Scones

Ingredients:

- 2 cups (250g) all-purpose flour
- ¼ cup (50g) sugar
- ¼ cup (25g) cocoa powder
- 1 tbsp baking powder
- ½ tsp salt
- ½ cup (115g) cold butter, cubed
- ½ cup (120ml) milk
- 1 tsp vanilla extract
- ½ cup (90g) chocolate chips

Instructions:

1. Preheat oven to 400°F (200°C). Line a baking sheet with parchment paper.
2. Mix flour, sugar, cocoa powder, baking powder, and salt.
3. Cut in butter until mixture resembles coarse crumbs.
4. Stir in milk, vanilla, and chocolate chips.
5. Shape into a circle and cut into wedges.
6. Bake for 15-18 minutes.

Chocolate Rugelach

Ingredients:

- 1 cup (225g) butter, softened
- 8 oz (225g) cream cheese, softened
- 2 cups (250g) flour
- ¼ cup (50g) sugar
- ½ cup (90g) melted chocolate
- 1 egg (for egg wash)

Instructions:

1. Mix butter, cream cheese, flour, and sugar into a dough.
2. Chill for 30 minutes.
3. Roll out, spread with melted chocolate, and cut into triangles.
4. Roll up from wide end to tip.
5. Brush with egg wash and bake at 350°F (175°C) for 20 minutes.

Chocolate Biscotti

Ingredients:

- 1¾ cups (220g) flour
- ½ cup (50g) cocoa powder
- 1 cup (200g) sugar
- 1 tsp baking powder
- 2 eggs
- 1 tsp vanilla extract
- ½ cup (90g) chocolate chips

Instructions:

1. Preheat oven to 350°F (175°C).
2. Mix flour, cocoa, sugar, and baking powder.
3. Add eggs and vanilla, mixing until combined.
4. Fold in chocolate chips.
5. Shape into logs and bake for 25 minutes.
6. Slice and bake again for 10 minutes.

Chocolate Bread Pudding

Ingredients:

- 4 cups (200g) bread cubes
- 2 cups (480ml) milk
- ½ cup (100g) sugar
- ½ cup (90g) chocolate chips
- 2 eggs
- 1 tsp vanilla extract

Instructions:

1. Preheat oven to 350°F (175°C).
2. Heat milk and chocolate until melted.
3. Whisk eggs, sugar, and vanilla.
4. Stir in chocolate mixture, then pour over bread cubes.
5. Let sit for 10 minutes, then bake for 30 minutes.

Chocolate Danish

Ingredients:

- 1 sheet puff pastry
- ½ cup (90g) chocolate chips
- 1 egg (for egg wash)

Instructions:

1. Preheat oven to 375°F (190°C).
2. Roll out puff pastry and cut into rectangles.
3. Place chocolate chips in the center.
4. Fold over and seal edges.
5. Brush with egg wash and bake for 15 minutes.

Chocolate Fudge Bars

Ingredients:

- 1½ cups (180g) flour
- ½ cup (50g) cocoa powder
- 1 cup (200g) sugar
- ½ tsp salt
- ½ cup (115g) butter, melted
- 2 eggs
- ½ cup (90g) chocolate chips

Instructions:

1. Preheat oven to 350°F (175°C).
2. Mix flour, cocoa, sugar, and salt.
3. Stir in melted butter and eggs.
4. Fold in chocolate chips.
5. Spread into a baking pan and bake for 25 minutes.

Chocolate Shortbread

Ingredients:

- 1 cup (225g) butter, softened
- ½ cup (100g) sugar
- 2 cups (250g) flour
- ¼ cup (25g) cocoa powder
- ½ tsp salt

Instructions:

1. Preheat oven to 325°F (160°C).
2. Mix butter and sugar until smooth.
3. Stir in flour, cocoa, and salt.
4. Shape into a rectangle and cut into bars.
5. Bake for 20-25 minutes.

Chocolate Whoopie Pies

Ingredients:

- 2 cups (250g) flour
- ½ cup (50g) cocoa powder
- 1 cup (200g) sugar
- 1 tsp baking soda
- ½ tsp salt
- ½ cup (115g) butter, softened
- 1 egg
- 1 tsp vanilla extract
- 1 cup (240ml) milk

Instructions:

1. Preheat oven to 350°F (175°C).
2. Mix flour, cocoa, sugar, baking soda, and salt.
3. Add butter, egg, vanilla, and milk, mixing well.
4. Scoop onto a baking sheet and bake for 10-12 minutes.
5. Fill with cream filling and sandwich together.

Chocolate Macarons

Ingredients:

- 1 cup (100g) almond flour
- 1¾ cups (200g) powdered sugar
- 2 tbsp (15g) cocoa powder
- 3 egg whites
- ¼ cup (50g) granulated sugar
- ½ tsp vanilla extract
- 4 oz (115g) melted chocolate (for ganache)
- ¼ cup (60ml) heavy cream

Instructions:

1. Sift almond flour, powdered sugar, and cocoa powder together.
2. Whip egg whites until foamy, then slowly add granulated sugar and whip to stiff peaks.
3. Fold in dry ingredients gently.
4. Pipe onto a parchment-lined baking sheet and let rest for 30 minutes.
5. Bake at 300°F (150°C) for 12-15 minutes.
6. Heat heavy cream and mix with melted chocolate to make ganache.
7. Fill macarons with ganache once cooled.

Chocolate Churros

Ingredients:

- 1 cup (240ml) water
- 2 tbsp (30g) butter
- 1 tbsp sugar
- 1 cup (125g) flour
- 1 egg
- ½ cup (90g) chocolate chips
- Oil for frying
- Cinnamon sugar for coating

Instructions:

1. Boil water, butter, and sugar.
2. Stir in flour and mix until smooth.
3. Let cool, then beat in egg.
4. Pipe into hot oil and fry until golden.
5. Toss in cinnamon sugar.
6. Melt chocolate chips and drizzle over churros.

Chocolate Pecan Pie

Ingredients:

- 1 unbaked pie crust
- 1 cup (200g) sugar
- 1 cup (240ml) corn syrup
- 3 eggs
- 2 tbsp (30g) butter, melted
- 1 tsp vanilla extract
- 1 cup (120g) pecans
- ½ cup (90g) chocolate chips

Instructions:

1. Preheat oven to 350°F (175°C).
2. Whisk sugar, corn syrup, eggs, butter, and vanilla together.
3. Stir in pecans and chocolate chips.
4. Pour into crust and bake for 50-55 minutes.

Chocolate Pavlova

Ingredients:

- 4 egg whites
- 1 cup (200g) sugar
- 2 tbsp (15g) cocoa powder
- 1 tsp vinegar
- ½ tsp vanilla extract
- 4 oz (115g) melted chocolate
- 1 cup (240ml) whipped cream

Instructions:

1. Preheat oven to 275°F (135°C).
2. Beat egg whites and sugar to stiff peaks.
3. Fold in cocoa powder, vinegar, and vanilla.
4. Spoon onto a baking sheet and bake for 60 minutes.
5. Cool, then top with whipped cream and melted chocolate.

Chocolate Madeleines

Ingredients:

- ½ cup (115g) butter, melted
- ¾ cup (100g) flour
- ¼ cup (25g) cocoa powder
- ½ tsp baking powder
- 2 eggs
- ½ cup (100g) sugar
- 1 tsp vanilla extract

Instructions:

1. Preheat oven to 375°F (190°C).
2. Mix flour, cocoa, and baking powder.
3. Beat eggs and sugar until fluffy, then add vanilla and melted butter.
4. Fold in dry ingredients.
5. Fill madeleine molds and bake for 10-12 minutes.

Chocolate Peanut Butter Bars

Ingredients:

- 1 cup (250g) peanut butter
- ½ cup (115g) butter, melted
- 1 cup (200g) powdered sugar
- 1½ cups (180g) crushed graham crackers
- 1 cup (180g) melted chocolate

Instructions:

1. Mix peanut butter, butter, powdered sugar, and graham crackers.
2. Press into a pan.
3. Pour melted chocolate on top.
4. Chill for 1 hour, then cut into bars.

Chocolate Truffle Tart

Ingredients:

- 1½ cups (180g) crushed cookies
- ¼ cup (56g) melted butter
- 8 oz (225g) dark chocolate, melted
- 1 cup (240ml) heavy cream
- ¼ cup (50g) sugar

Instructions:

1. Preheat oven to 350°F (175°C).
2. Mix cookies and butter, press into tart pan, and bake for 10 minutes.
3. Heat cream and sugar, then mix with melted chocolate.
4. Pour into crust and chill for 2 hours.

Chocolate Meringue Pie

Ingredients:

- 1 pre-baked pie crust
- 1 cup (240ml) milk
- ½ cup (100g) sugar
- ¼ cup (25g) cocoa powder
- 2 tbsp cornstarch
- 2 egg yolks
- ½ tsp vanilla extract
- 3 egg whites
- ¼ cup (50g) sugar (for meringue)

Instructions:

1. Heat milk, sugar, cocoa, and cornstarch, stirring until thick.
2. Stir in egg yolks and vanilla.
3. Pour into crust.
4. Beat egg whites with sugar until stiff peaks form.
5. Spread meringue over pie and bake at 350°F (175°C) for 10 minutes.

Chocolate Torte

Ingredients:

- 6 oz (170g) dark chocolate, melted
- ½ cup (115g) butter
- ¾ cup (150g) sugar
- 4 eggs
- ½ cup (60g) flour

Instructions:

1. Preheat oven to 350°F (175°C).
2. Beat butter and sugar until fluffy.
3. Add eggs one at a time, then mix in melted chocolate and flour.
4. Pour into a greased pan and bake for 25 minutes.

Chocolate Zucchini Bread

Ingredients:

- 1½ cups (190g) flour
- ½ cup (50g) cocoa powder
- 1 tsp baking powder
- 1 tsp baking soda
- ½ tsp salt
- 1 tsp cinnamon
- 2 eggs
- 1 cup (200g) sugar
- ½ cup (120ml) vegetable oil
- 1 tsp vanilla extract
- 1 cup (130g) grated zucchini
- ½ cup (90g) chocolate chips

Instructions:

1. Preheat oven to 350°F (175°C). Grease a loaf pan.
2. Mix dry ingredients together.
3. Whisk eggs, sugar, oil, and vanilla.
4. Stir in grated zucchini and chocolate chips.
5. Fold in dry ingredients and pour into the pan.
6. Bake for 55-60 minutes, or until a toothpick comes out clean.

Chocolate Sticky Buns

Ingredients:

- 2 cups (250g) flour
- 1 packet active dry yeast
- ½ cup (120ml) warm milk
- ¼ cup (50g) sugar
- ¼ cup (60g) butter, softened
- 1 egg
- ½ tsp salt
- ½ cup (100g) brown sugar
- ½ cup (120ml) heavy cream
- ½ cup (90g) chocolate chips

Instructions:

1. Preheat oven to 350°F (175°C).
2. Combine yeast, warm milk, and sugar; let sit for 5 minutes.
3. Mix in butter, egg, salt, and flour, knead until smooth.
4. Let dough rise for 1 hour.
5. Roll dough out and sprinkle with brown sugar, chocolate chips, and cinnamon.
6. Roll up dough, slice into buns, and place in a greased pan.
7. Pour heavy cream over buns and bake for 25-30 minutes.

Chocolate Bread

Ingredients:

- 1½ cups (190g) flour
- ½ cup (50g) cocoa powder
- 1 tsp baking powder
- 1 tsp salt
- 1 cup (200g) sugar
- 2 eggs
- ½ cup (120ml) milk
- ½ cup (115g) butter, melted
- 1 tsp vanilla extract
- ½ cup (90g) chocolate chips

Instructions:

1. Preheat oven to 350°F (175°C). Grease a loaf pan.
2. Mix dry ingredients together.
3. Whisk eggs, milk, butter, and vanilla.
4. Combine wet and dry ingredients, then fold in chocolate chips.
5. Pour into the pan and bake for 45-50 minutes.

Chocolate Crinkle Cookies

Ingredients:

- 1½ cups (190g) flour
- ¾ cup (75g) cocoa powder
- 1 tsp baking powder
- ½ tsp salt
- 2 eggs
- 1 cup (200g) sugar
- ½ cup (115g) butter, softened
- 1 tsp vanilla extract
- ½ cup (50g) powdered sugar

Instructions:

1. Preheat oven to 350°F (175°C). Line baking sheet with parchment.
2. Mix flour, cocoa, baking powder, and salt.
3. Beat eggs, sugar, butter, and vanilla until fluffy.
4. Gradually add dry ingredients, then chill dough for 30 minutes.
5. Roll dough into balls, coat in powdered sugar, and bake for 10-12 minutes.

Chocolate Almond Cake

Ingredients:

- 1 cup (120g) flour
- ½ cup (50g) cocoa powder
- 1 tsp baking powder
- ½ tsp baking soda
- ½ tsp salt
- 1 cup (200g) sugar
- 2 eggs
- 1 tsp vanilla extract
- 1 cup (240ml) almond milk
- ½ cup (115g) butter, softened
- ½ cup (50g) sliced almonds

Instructions:

1. Preheat oven to 350°F (175°C). Grease and flour a cake pan.
2. Mix dry ingredients together.
3. Beat sugar, eggs, butter, and vanilla.
4. Add dry ingredients alternately with almond milk.
5. Pour into pan and bake for 30-35 minutes.
6. Top with almonds and bake for an additional 5 minutes.

Chocolate Marbled Pound Cake

Ingredients:

- 2 cups (250g) flour
- 1 tsp baking powder
- ¼ tsp salt
- 1 cup (225g) butter, softened
- 1 cup (200g) sugar
- 4 eggs
- 1 tsp vanilla extract
- ½ cup (120ml) milk
- 2 oz (55g) melted dark chocolate

Instructions:

1. Preheat oven to 350°F (175°C). Grease and flour a loaf pan.
2. Mix flour, baking powder, and salt together.
3. Cream butter and sugar, then beat in eggs one at a time.
4. Add dry ingredients alternately with milk.
5. Split the batter in half, mixing melted chocolate into one half.
6. Pour both batters into the pan and swirl with a knife.
7. Bake for 60 minutes or until a toothpick comes out clean.

Chocolate Biscuit Cake

Ingredients:

- 8 oz (225g) digestive biscuits
- 1 cup (200g) chocolate chips
- ¼ cup (60g) butter
- 2 tbsp honey
- ¼ cup (60ml) heavy cream

Instructions:

1. Crush biscuits into small pieces.
2. Melt chocolate, butter, honey, and cream in a double boiler.
3. Pour melted mixture over biscuits and mix well.
4. Press into a greased pan and refrigerate for 2 hours.
5. Slice and serve chilled.

Chocolate Roll Cake

Ingredients:

- ¾ cup (95g) all-purpose flour
- ¼ cup (25g) cocoa powder
- 1 tsp baking powder
- ¼ tsp salt
- 4 eggs
- ¾ cup (150g) sugar
- 1 tsp vanilla extract
- 1 cup (240ml) whipped cream

Instructions:

1. Preheat oven to 375°F (190°C). Line a baking sheet with parchment paper.
2. Whisk flour, cocoa powder, baking powder, and salt.
3. Beat eggs and sugar until thick and pale, then fold in dry ingredients.
4. Spread batter onto pan and bake for 10-12 minutes.
5. Once cooled, roll cake with a towel, then unroll and spread with whipped cream.
6. Roll up again and chill before serving.

Chocolate Cupcakes

Ingredients:

- 1¾ cups (220g) flour
- ¾ cup (75g) cocoa powder
- 1 tsp baking powder
- 1 tsp baking soda
- ½ tsp salt
- 1 cup (200g) sugar
- 2 eggs
- 1 tsp vanilla extract
- 1 cup (240ml) milk
- ½ cup (115g) butter, melted

Instructions:

1. Preheat oven to 350°F (175°C). Line muffin tins with cupcake liners.
2. Mix dry ingredients together.
3. Beat eggs, sugar, butter, and vanilla.
4. Add dry ingredients alternately with milk.
5. Pour batter into liners and bake for 18-20 minutes.

Chocolate Oatmeal Cookies

Ingredients:

- 1 cup (90g) oats
- ¾ cup (95g) flour
- ½ tsp baking soda
- ½ tsp salt
- 1 tsp cinnamon
- ½ cup (115g) butter, softened
- 1 cup (200g) brown sugar
- 1 egg
- 1 tsp vanilla extract
- 1 cup (180g) chocolate chips

Instructions:

1. Preheat oven to 350°F (175°C). Line a baking sheet with parchment paper.
2. Mix flour, oats, baking soda, salt, and cinnamon.
3. Cream butter and brown sugar, then beat in egg and vanilla.
4. Stir in dry ingredients, then fold in chocolate chips.
5. Drop spoonfuls of dough onto the baking sheet and bake for 10-12 minutes.

Chocolate Banana Bread

Ingredients:

- 2 ripe bananas, mashed
- 1½ cups (190g) flour
- ½ cup (50g) cocoa powder
- 1 tsp baking soda
- ¼ tsp salt
- ½ cup (100g) sugar
- ½ cup (120ml) vegetable oil
- 2 eggs
- 1 tsp vanilla extract
- ½ cup (90g) chocolate chips

Instructions:

1. Preheat oven to 350°F (175°C). Grease a loaf pan.
2. Mash bananas and mix with sugar, eggs, oil, and vanilla.
3. In another bowl, combine flour, cocoa powder, baking soda, and salt.
4. Stir dry ingredients into wet mixture, then fold in chocolate chips.
5. Pour into the pan and bake for 55-60 minutes.

Chocolate Pretzel Bites

Ingredients:

- 1 bag mini pretzels
- 1 cup (170g) chocolate chips
- ½ cup (90g) M&M's (optional)

Instructions:

1. Preheat oven to 350°F (175°C). Line a baking sheet with parchment paper.
2. Place pretzels on the baking sheet in a single layer.
3. Melt chocolate chips in a microwave-safe bowl, stirring every 30 seconds.
4. Spoon melted chocolate over each pretzel and top with M&M's if desired.
5. Chill in the fridge for 30 minutes to set.

Chocolate Puff Pastry Twists

Ingredients:

- 1 sheet puff pastry (store-bought)
- ¼ cup (50g) chocolate chips
- 1 tbsp sugar (optional)
- 1 egg (for egg wash)

Instructions:

1. Preheat oven to 375°F (190°C). Line a baking sheet with parchment paper.
2. Roll out puff pastry and spread chocolate chips evenly over one half.
3. Fold pastry over the chocolate and press to seal.
4. Cut into strips and twist each strip into a spiral.
5. Brush with egg wash and sprinkle with sugar if desired.
6. Bake for 15-18 minutes until golden and puffed.

Chocolate Bundt Cake

Ingredients:

- 2 cups (250g) flour
- 1 cup (200g) sugar
- ½ cup (50g) cocoa powder
- 1 tsp baking powder
- 1 tsp baking soda
- ½ tsp salt
- 2 eggs
- 1 cup (240ml) milk
- ½ cup (120g) butter, softened
- 1 tsp vanilla extract
- ½ cup (120ml) boiling water
- 1 cup (180g) chocolate chips

Instructions:

1. Preheat oven to 350°F (175°C). Grease a Bundt pan.
2. In a bowl, mix dry ingredients together.
3. Beat eggs, milk, butter, and vanilla.
4. Gradually add dry ingredients, mixing until smooth.
5. Stir in chocolate chips and pour into the pan.
6. Bake for 35-40 minutes.

Chocolate Cinnamon Rolls

Ingredients:

- 1 package (2½ tsp) active dry yeast
- ¾ cup (180ml) warm milk
- ½ cup (100g) sugar
- 1/3 cup (75g) butter, softened
- 2 eggs
- 4 cups (500g) flour
- ½ tsp salt
- ½ cup (50g) cocoa powder
- 1 tsp cinnamon
- ½ cup (100g) chocolate chips
- 1 cup (240ml) heavy cream

Instructions:

1. Preheat oven to 350°F (175°C). Grease a baking dish.
2. Mix yeast, warm milk, and 1 tbsp sugar; let sit for 5 minutes.
3. Combine butter, eggs, remaining sugar, salt, and flour in a bowl.
4. Add yeast mixture and knead dough for 5-7 minutes. Let rise for 1 hour.
5. Roll dough into a rectangle, spread with cocoa powder, cinnamon, and chocolate chips.
6. Roll up dough, slice into rolls, and place in the dish.
7. Pour cream over the rolls and bake for 25-30 minutes.

Chocolate Raspberry Bars

Ingredients:

- 1 cup (120g) flour
- 1/2 cup (50g) cocoa powder
- 1 tsp baking powder
- ½ tsp salt
- 1 cup (200g) sugar
- 1 egg
- 1 tsp vanilla extract
- ½ cup (120g) butter, softened
- 1/2 cup (120g) raspberry jam
- 1/2 cup (90g) chocolate chips

Instructions:

1. Preheat oven to 350°F (175°C). Grease a baking dish.
2. Mix flour, cocoa powder, baking powder, and salt.
3. Beat butter and sugar, then add egg and vanilla.
4. Gradually add dry ingredients and mix until combined.
5. Spread the dough in the dish, then swirl raspberry jam over the top.
6. Sprinkle chocolate chips on top and bake for 20-25 minutes.

Chocolate Dipped Biscotti

Ingredients:

- 1½ cups (190g) flour
- ½ tsp baking powder
- ½ tsp salt
- 1 cup (200g) sugar
- 2 eggs
- 1 tsp vanilla extract
- 1 cup (160g) chocolate chips

Instructions:

1. Preheat oven to 350°F (175°C). Line a baking sheet with parchment paper.
2. Mix dry ingredients together.
3. Beat eggs, sugar, and vanilla, then gradually add dry ingredients.
4. Shape dough into a log and bake for 25-30 minutes.
5. Slice into biscotti and bake for an additional 10-12 minutes.
6. Dip cooled biscotti into melted chocolate and let set.

Chocolate Marshmallow Brownies

Ingredients:

- 1 cup (200g) sugar
- ½ cup (115g) butter, melted
- 2 eggs
- 1 tsp vanilla extract
- ¾ cup (95g) flour
- ½ cup (50g) cocoa powder
- ½ tsp baking powder
- ½ tsp salt
- 1½ cups (170g) mini marshmallows
- ½ cup (90g) chocolate chips

Instructions:

1. Preheat oven to 350°F (175°C). Grease a baking dish.
2. Mix melted butter, sugar, eggs, and vanilla.
3. Add flour, cocoa powder, baking powder, and salt.
4. Fold in chocolate chips, then pour batter into the dish.
5. Bake for 20-25 minutes, then top with marshmallows.
6. Bake for an additional 5-10 minutes until marshmallows are golden.

www.ingramcontent.com/pod-product-compliance
Lightning Source LLC
LaVergne TN
LVHW081324060526
838201LV00055B/2441